Journey
with Job

Journey with Job

Thomas John Carlisle

Wm. B. Eerdmans Publishing Company
Grand Rapids

Library of Congress Cataloging in Publication Data

Carlisle, Thomas John.
Journey with Job.
I. Title.
PS3553.A73J6   811'.5'4   75-34230
ISBN 0-8028-1617-7

ACKNOWLEDGMENTS

The author wishes to thank the following publications, in whose pages certain of these poems first appeared, for permission to include them in this book:

AMERICAN WEAVE: "I talked with Job."

THE CHRISTIAN CENTURY: "Happy Ending."

CHRISTIAN HERALD. Copyright 1970 by Christian Herald Association, Inc.: "Superior Comforter," "Beside Me," "Target," "My Sin Is Ever Before Me," "Songs in the Night," "If Only," "Though He Slay Me," "And Job Replied," "Another Ashpit," "The Glory," "The Name of Job."

ENQUIRY. Copyright 1973 by Geneva Press; copyright transferred to Thomas John Carlisle 1974: "Author, Author," "Remainder," "Hers Too," "What Job Really Said," "What's in a Name," "A Football for His Friends," "Advice," "The Trick's on You," "Complaint to the Almighty," "What Use?" "In My Judgment," "In His Crucible," "Sit Tight," "Illusions of Logic," "Off Key," "No Doubt," "Sum and Substance," "The Gift I Need," "Basic Question," "Requiem," "The Sterility of Morality," "Credit," "Prudent, Practical, and Profitable," "Eulogy," "Footnote to Job's Eulogy," "Second Footnote," "I Need to Know," "Multiple Offender," "The Eloquence of Elihu," "Impaled," "Defenders of the Faith," "Which God?" "Good Grit," "Choice," "A Word In," "All We Hear," "Please Touch," "I Trust You, God," "What He Needed," "Ransomed," "Bondsman," "Disbelief," "Extension," "If a Man Die," "Intimation of Immortality," "Amazing," "Like a Small Job," "Psalm," "Putting It All Together," "Job's Question Over Again," "There Was a Man," "By Faith," "Did He?" "Haunted and Taunted," "This Day," Cosmic Clues," "Intellection," "When God Replies," "Whirlwind Courtship," "Out of the Whirlwind," "God's Power Play," "Logistics," "Interview," "After the Ashpit."

FRIENDS JOURNAL. Copyright 1971 by Friends Publishing Company: "Hide and Seek." Copyright 1972 by Friends Publishing Company: "More Words," "Expositor."

KANSAS CITY STAR: "Portrait," "Phenomenon," "Hardly Job."

PRESBYTERIAN LIFE. Copyright 1969 by Presbyterian Life, Inc.: "Alpha and Omega," "Gracious Living," "In the Ashpit," "Given and Taken," "Could I?" Copyright 1970 by Presbyterian Life, Inc.: "Why?"

SATURDAY REVIEW. Copyright 1970 by Saturday Review, Inc.: "Job's Wife."

The illustrations used on the cover and throughout this book are the property of the American Bible Society, and are used with permission of the Society.

Contents

1 author of Job

Author, Author

To what extent
is this most brilliant book
more than biography
more than a drama
more than a puissant poem
more than an essay
on morals or philosophy
(or, if not more, then, other)?

Try its substance
with your mind's finger
and find the autograph
the personal profile
memoirs of a man
confessing to the world
and to himself
and inferentially to One
without whom world and self
would not be words at all.

How shall we christen
this anonymous
scribe of our saga
blood brother to the blows
of struggle and storm
which bend our backs
and twist our heads
and leave us writhing
wounded and yet aware
of sentience
and the worth
of being one?

Alpha and Omega

In the beginning it was Job
and in the end it was Job
the broken
the breaker of silence
the unembittered
but the brash
challenger of Omnipotence
who knew wherewith
and whomwith
his beginning
and his ending
were.

2 meet Job

Gracious Living

There was a man
whose origin was God
whose name was Job
who lived down east
who made it to the top
and who supposed
that his high potency
and his proliferation
of capital
and progeny
and all his large
and little luxuries
were due
to his outstanding
character and class
so due him too
thank God
which he remembered
in his prayers.
He had good reason
for the high regard
that God
and men
and even his wife
accorded him
and all went well
until two damning days
which totally demolished
his outward
and his inward
euphoria.

In the Ashpit

He was a sad spectacle
a dark eyesore
sitting in that ashpit
his unhappy skin
tattooed with ulcers
ugly as the sin
he had not sinned.
Unrecognizable
even to his severest
friends but for the fact
he was the only one
with that affliction
out back
of that address.
An ominous advertisement
for the just deserts
and guaranteed remuneration
of generosity
integrity
and innocence.
A tainted testimonial
to cosmic justice.

Given and Taken

This was not the first
of Job's concurrent crises.
One demonic day
a most cacophonous
quartet of couriers
came in on various notes
to vocalize
his hideous
and sorcerous
catastrophes.

Fresh from the field
the first reported
that all Job's jeeps
            and tractors
(oxen and asses
in this instance)
were stolen by Sabeans.
But such can be replaced.

Next came the informant
with the news flash
that lightning
had struck his safe
and cremated his stocks
and all his securities
(the modern equivalent
of thundering herds
and prolific flocks).
A bitter blow
but not a knockout.

The third was the puffing
and panting announcer
crying that three bands
of churlish Chaldeans
had rounded up Job's jaguars
his cadillacs

and all his personal planes
(actually and more accurately
his fleet of speedy camels)
and sent them flying
for parts unknown.
But one can walk
without a camel
or a sports car
and more
can be assembled.

He was still speaking
when another came
and gasping interrupted
the previous
annunciator of bad tidings
to tell of a tornado
that crumbled the penthouse
where all Job's sons
and all Job's daughters
were merrily dining
and none escaped
from the twister's misery
except this flushed
hysterical
and overeager
herald of havoc.

That was a day
to howl at heaven
and curse the earth
but Job took it:

> *The Lord has given.*
> *The Lord has taken.*
> *He is still my God.*

3 Job's wife

Job's Wife

Job's wife is often caricatured
as a second Satan since she said
"Curse God and die," though few would like
to have their own biography encapsuled
in one phrase in or out of context.
At least she didn't prostitute theology
and make believe to dust her husband's ashpit.

We don't know whether she brought out snacks
or started a barbecue to feed his friends
who were so hungry to devour him.

Perhaps she had to take a job
to shield herself from the poorhouse and provide
for doctor's bills—if one would come—
and to take her mind off what the patient looked like
and all that had happened to her as well as him.

Job did not cry which doesn't mean she didn't.

It's hard to have a hero for a husband.

Remainder

She stayed—God bless her—shared
in all that bugged her husband.
His hang-up was her hang-up too.

Hers Too

Whose children were they who so instantly
stopped eating and stopped drinking and
          stopped living?
Not Job's alone by any manner of means!

What Job Really Said

He did not brand her as a silly fool
but only said right then she talked like one
and tenderly postscripted it with *we*
regarding good and poor reception
from God's disposals.

4 *Job's children—before*

Father Job

I talked with Job
and asked him whether he made it
too easy for his children
with all the lavish
and the luxury
available from his
diversified
portfolios.

He thought it over
said I had a point
that he would ponder further
though now it was too late
to alter their education.

Then he added:
Praying is not enough—
or sacrificing.
And yet whatever
a father gives
devoid of prayer
devoid of sacrifice
is little enough
and less than little.

Devastated

Was he devastated
by their death
or quietly
unruffled?
Did he register
the customary
appropriate
requirements
for mourning
but choose
not to expose
the nerve ends
of his naked
aching sorrow?

5 Job's friends

What's in a Name ?

God crushes is what *Eliphaz'*
name means. God crushes sinners:
which meant *he* went uncrushed
while spreading his serene
and tireless word
that suffering is after all
most just and logical
the apt reward for sin.

Bildad never doubted
that *darling of God*
was apropos for him
though not for Job
whose sons' delinquencies
must have brought down
the house upon their heads.
and implicated
their parent in the bargain.

Zophar was sorely irked
to be reminded
his name spelled *twittering bird*
or *jumping goat*
or *a sharp nail*
since none communicated
his humorless
opinion of himself
or his acuity
as just accuser—
except the nail!

Welcome in this case
the friends whose words
provoke the terror
and the majesty
of Job's replies:
Eliphaz, Bildad, Zophar
you live—
because of Job.

Superior Comforter

It is a large order
for friends to stay
shut up.
    And Job was
no luckier than we.
It is the subtle
and grateful
superiority
of the nonsufferer
that gets us.
He is glad
that he isn't in
our boat
but he bids us
keep an elevated chin
and not rock anything.
He knows
he can go home
unscathed
not being
at our address
or in our shoes.
Let him screw
his own courage
to the sticking place
when the time comes.

Beside Me

Sit on the ground beside me.
Your arguments
can come later
your ingenious
or specious
exegesis
for my tragic
condition.
But sit on the ground
beside me now
and weep with me
until my woe
flows over.
Bottle my tears
for a rainy day.

A Football for His Friends

They meant him well
despite their poisoned words—
or thought they did
and thought those words benign.
After the silence
of grand sympathy
they let their specious proverbs
flow like wine
along with other wisdom
which their friend
was in no frame or mood
to treat with grace.
They did not know
their platitudes were rude
irrelevant.
They were not forced to face
the frenzy of his world
stripped raw, bereft
of all that furnished
shelter, ease, and mirth
and peace of mind and body.
He became
a toy—a target—
for both heaven and earth.

The Ashpit Hearings

Job's friends
gathered at the ashpit
and conducted hearings
with loaded questions
and aloof concern
for their upended
associate and superior.

He looked for a lawyer
when the heat was on
but found no advocate
in his immediate vicinity
but kept on looking.

He appealed
to a higher court
than they could recognize.
They overheard his pleas
but could not face them.
They quoted old textbooks
irrelevant revelations.
They witnessed without wit
or wisdom but a wry
and melancholy reading.
They cried circumstantial
evidence as damning
and thought he better
throw himself on the mercy
they clearly did not have
and could not contemplate
or fathom.

All their sentences
were harsh but not unusual.

6 constant confrontation

Target

Drunk with his pain
Job dared and dared again
to parry the arrows
of prim and pious
religiosity
expressed with the best
flourishes
and scripts lush
with spare platitudes.
But still the haunting hurt
remained unstilled:
>Why me?
>*Why me?*
>**WHY ME?**
>the sitting target
>for the Omnipotent
>>Archer.

Advice

Good Job could not believe
that God would not regret
his permanent passing.
>Hide me somewhere
>until with second thoughts
>you think of me.
>Even you
>must find friends few.

The Trick's on You

Some morning, God,
when I occur to you,
you will discover
that I am no longer
discoverable.
Suppose I have
sinned   how
could that hurt you?
You must have something
        better
to do than scrutinize
my scrofulence.
Let me spit
or swallow my spittle
without your spying.

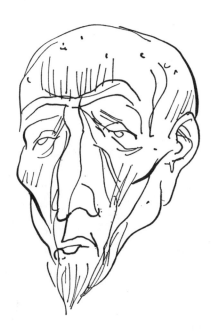

Complaint to the Almighty

You hang around
too faithfully.

What Use?

What use is any man
to God being so little
use to himself?

Why?

O God, why
have you swept me under
the carpet like dirt
interred in the least
remarkable manner?
Why, O God,
have you curbed my joy
and accelerated
my pain?
I am sick
and tired
in more ways
than two.
Is there a good reason
or did it just happen
while you were occupied
with other children's business?

In My Judgment

What shall I require
of the omnivorous Prowler?
How make him testify
to his strange habits
which fail to wash
in my analysis?
Even if he will not
give me a hearing
I will arrange
a day in court for him.

In His Crucible

Eastward I go
and find him not at home.
Westward I wander
seeing no more of him.
Equator, Cancer,
Capricorn, and Pole
make him no less
invisible.
But every step of mine
is in his glass
and all my sin
is magnified
and marked.

7 *large logic and small comfort*

Sit Tight

God's secret service
should provide
maximum security
for all who toe his line.
According to logic
angels should enact
a swoop of Superman
to set you safe
where devils fear to tread.
God will not let you down
as long as you
aspire to hold him up.
Tick off your fears:
frost, drought, ferocity
of hungry predators,
tight money,
stingy creditors,
the tongue's lash,
cruelest tools of war—
but then sit tight
inside your armored vehicle
of rectitude
and inexperience.

Illusions of Logic

Man contrives
many of his own troubles.
Some griefs grow
from spite we sow—
our spate of truculence.
Adversity has profitable
lessons for the studious.
The one who wounds
soothes with a surer hand—
sometimes and under certain
circumstances.
If I were you
does not turn you to me.
When my turn comes—
perish the thought, of course—
I may lose patience too—
and more than patience!

Off Key

Sweet nothings
of scant comfort
sound melodious
principally to the speaker.

No Doubt

O God,
sit still
so we can study you
observe
dissect
and analyze
what makes you
tick, what made you
in the first place.
Do not writhe
at our contortions.
We are scientists
and hope to open
a heaven of knowledge
by these disquisitions.
Once we have put you
in your place no doubt
our efforts will save you
for an incredulous world.

Sum and Substance

It is my own body
about which I am most
immediately
and compassionately
concerned
touched
prioritied.
I feel
affectionately
and totally
for myself:
my grief
my pain
my delight
my joy.
My kingdom
has boundaries
demarcated
by my silhouette.
My skeleton
and my flesh
engross
obsess
monopolize
my care.

The Gift I Need

Pity me.
Pity me.
Pity me.
Listen
only
listen.
Do not pursue me
as though you were God.
The gift I need
is your hearing
and your heart.

Basic Question

I talked with Job
and asked him how he learned
to talk with God.

8 *the sterility of moralism*

Requiem

And all recalls us to the death we die:
the sonics of the bee's frustrated buzz
upon the pane which will not let him by,
the spider's lustrous filaments, the blue
and shattered egg no longer in the nest,
no longer viable, the broken best
of Wedgwood and majolica, the new
we welcome and discard, the obsolete
which animates no obsequies, the crude,
the crass, the twisted, and the incomplete,
the mouths that never find a full day's food,
the boils and unjust turmoils known in Uz,
and one lying in state who is not I.

The Sterility of Morality

I knock
and say:
       Your hospitality
       (heaven, if you prefer
       to name your domicile)
       is obligated
       by my excellence
       innocence
       integrity
       and other attributes
       too numerous to mention.
       Open up!

Credit

I think that God
should give me
a separate receipt
and "thank you"
each time I go
an extra foot or two
or dole a hard-earned dollar
from my cache.

Prudent, Practical and Profitable

I talked with Job
and asked him his techniques
for positive thinking
peace of mind
and preservation
of our wise way of life.
Confident as I was
that God—
or is it Satan?—
prefers our pious
acquiescence
and pays us
promptly and in kind
for all our snuffling
and our sniffling.
But Job demurred.

My Sin Is Ever Before Me

God need not
say O.K.
to my day's doings.
If he did
I might assume
I made it
by myself
and could engrave
another star
on my eternal chart.
No hole in one,
no home run
with the bases
loaded with friends,
no mile in less
than four,
no hundred-yard
touchdown
can qualify me
to tell him off
or label him
as surplus.

Eulogy

Job's catalog
of civic virtues
and commendable
compassion
for those who did not have
his wisdom
or his wealth
or his good luck
(prior to his present
raw deal
and rotten hand)
resembles
a suitable
though fulsome
testimonial
from someone else
which might
have made him blush
had he been listener
rather than speaker.

Footnote to Job's Eulogy

I can list
almost as many
meritorious—
and, modestly—
magnanimous
magnificent
conspicuous
phenomenal
and unbelievable
abilities
and attributes
I happen
to possess.

Second Footnote

On second thought
I think
I have good reason
to keep quiet
regarding
the multiplicity
of my imaginary
altruisms.

I Need to Know

And yet I need to know
what constitutes
the "doing justly"
and the "loving mercy"
which the prophet praised
along with "walking humbly."
Job's long checklist
gives me strings
for every finger
and remembrancers
of what it means
to take Christ at his word
on the necessity
and joy
of finding
and of loving
my elusive "neighbors."

Multiple Offender

Job was offensive
to his wife
    though she stood by
    in silence
    following her frank advice
and to his friends
    defensive in contrived
    and lengthy briefs
    exonerating God
and to those readers
    of his hot wild words
    who thought them
      blasphemous
    and tried to ban
    his book from the Boston
    of their Bible
and to us
    because it hurts
    to admit our Deity
    is a poor paymaster
    and an enigmatist.

Portrait

I shall not call him Job.
His troubles
bubbled and boiled
from cauldrons
of his venom.
He could be kind.
His face relaxed
when stopping to think
of beauty and the proof
its presence provided
for a proper God.
He could refute
the choicest refutations
and establish
his propositions
and presuppositions
as divinely etched
without divine assistance
or compassion.
And he was right
and rigid
and righteous.
And no one pitied
the hell
which he created
for himself
since it was good
enough for him.

9 *the fourth friend*

A Late Starter

Elihu was a late
starter. The scorecard
omits his name.
Three veteran pitchers
had hurled their hardest
without getting Job out.
And now from the stands
this freshman rookie
strides to the mound
to put one over
for God. His warmup
is deliberate—
a neophyte trying
to justify
his stance and position.
He fails to retire
Job but he clearly
puts one strike over.
Don't miss it!

The Eloquence of Elihu

Since you have failed—you three—
though older and presumably
wiser than I—you forfeit
your chance to vindicate
the Lord. Leave it to me.
I mark the loopholes Job
has squeezed through cunningly.
I'll close them while I talk—
and talk—and talk—and talk.

More Words

There are always more words
for God. We are willing
to provide them unasked.
We arrogate power
of attorney, preempt
his time and his program
and expect gratitude
for moving big fat mouths.
Still we might learn to be still.

Expositor

On God's behalf
I am not first
nor last to speak.
In my own bag
are many trinkets.
Some are labeled WISDOM.
Some I should discard
considering they fail
to fit the facts.
I love to hear
my voice composing
arias of arid
philosophy in beautiful
cadenzas. The applause
I give myself
is devastating.

Impaled

The arrogance
of my ignorance
impales me
on my own
philosophy.

Songs in the Night

The hidden God
composes songs
for me.
And I can listen
when I cannot
see.

Because of the Darkness

Because of the darkness
we find it hard
to argue with God.
We cannot confuse him
by our confusion.
In all our affliction
his love may not be obvious
but not oblivious either.
So much the better
for us.

Unexpected Response

My cry
was God's answer.

Uncovery

My ear was uncovered
when I struggled to hear
my own complaints.
A mixed blessing
for then I heard
the troubles of others
which compared favorably
with mine.

Defenders of the Faith

We make God guilty
in the minds of many
and peel Him down
to apparent impotence
and imbecility
when we consider ourselves
defense attorneys
for the Almighty.
Better share
a little of his love
and demonstrate—
but not debate
or denigrate—
his human interest.

10 which God?

Which God?

Job was tortured
by the abyss between
the god who manipulates
and The God who sustains.
He saw good fortune
go out the window
and down the drain
and under the rainbow
he couldn't see
for searching his soul
for cause and effect
and pay me my wages.
But what am I saying?
My guilt-edged goodness
is hardly a head start
on heaven or happiness.
Somewhere His Highness
has something closer
to bonds of friendship
no matter how costly
the uninsurance
that goes with grace.

Good Grit

The God who appeared
to turn his back
on suffering
and contentious
Job
counted
on Job
for faith
and grit
and perseverance.

Phenomenon

The demise
of the divine
matches the heresy
of those who paint
God with their own
        stiff brush
of humorless
dispassion.
God knows how
to set winds blowing
and when most at rest
invigorates
creation.

Choice

What kind
of unkind God
unkin to man
am I allowed
to find
in literature
or life?
One who can match
subjects with Satan?
One who can listen
momentarily
to man?
One who can climb
down out of heaven
and up a tortured hill?
This is a mystery
story and a saga.
I read
I run
and I decide
for deicide
or for disciple-ing.

A Word In

Silence is not
without sound
I hear
the nearer waters
of the world
the dew descending
the dead-end fly
mosquito small talk
incipient rain
the sighs of trees
the shivering of grass
the click of stones
a throbbing plane
and God
getting a word in
sidewise
edgewise
crosswise.

All We Hear

A whisper and an echo
in the unlighted dark
is all we hear—
except for when he thunders!

Please Touch

God, you are not
away off there
in some anywhere.
For me you are
smiling in my love
for someone
with whom
I almost failed
to pass the time
of day. Help me
touch you when I
touch others
ever so slightly.

Hide and Seek

You whom I hide from
even while I am protesting
that you are evading
me, your origin
and your accomplishments
tingle all my senses
and flow through the tangled
patterns of my cerebral
apparatus. Why should I
discard you for lack of
an identification label
or because all names I give
serve to belittle you?

I Trust You God *(Job's Theological Argument)*

You promised,
covenanted.
Keep your contract.

Noah saw
your bow
and knew it colored
all futures.

Abraham
heard your word
believed it
and remembered.

Jacob
wrestled
until you
blessed him.

And Moses
turned aside
to take
you affidavit.

You can't go back
on promises—
not you.
I might and do.

You can't deny
yourself or you
are blotted out
and we as well.

By God
I judge you, God,
and you must listen
to yourself
if not to me.

11 *intimations of hope*

What He Needed

To bridge the abyss
was more than even
heroic Job
could hope to achieve.
He tried with his tirades
his claims and arguments
the righteousness he arrogated
his deeds of rectitude
and lovingkindness
to build his Babel
and to scale the summit
of Sovereignty beyond
the reach of mortal man.

He gasped at last
and cried
for an arbiter
and daysman
an ombudsman
an advocate
to plead his case
a Bridge-Man
to span the chasm
of estrangement.
Yes, he knew
what he needed.

If Only

No wonder that we cry:
        If only I
        knew where to address him
        how to ring his doorbell
        how to breach
        the bastions
        of omnipotent mystery.
If only.
Only if.

Ransomed

Hostage to God's justice
Job endured
pain's pistols
doubt's blindfold
and the cords
of unrequited love.
And in exchange
conceived the dream
of a redeemer.

Bondsman

Since no one cares
to set his hand
on mine
as surety
my only guarantor
is God.

Disbelief

I cannot believe
O God
I cannot believe
that you will leave me
orphan in your world
or let me be
at my long last
no more.

Extension

O God
our dialogue
incipient now
might be continued
beneficially
if you extend my lease
past my obituary.

Though He Slay Me

Most of my time I spend
suffering. There is no end
to the weight nerves can find
to channel to the raw mind.
Faithfully I try to disperse
their legions. I traverse
a universe of grace
searching for the eternal face
of love and, finding none,
hold on, hold on, hold on.

If a Man Die

You will not let me go
O God
now in my hardship
and harassment.

Will you relax your grip
when death demands?
Or do you care?

Or do you care!

Intimation of Immortality

Out of the depths
of pain and the pessimism
which exacerbated
his anguish
Job prayed
and then impertinently proposed
the possibility
that man's long sleep
might be susceptible
to God's invasion.

Amazing

Amazing was the grace
which gifted Job
and lifted the dead weight
of that long malaise
compounded by his pain
his brain's raw questions
and his cruel estrangement
from those he counted intimates
including God.

How sweet the sound
of morning stars
and shouts of joy
from other heavenly bodies.
More sweet to him
his confrontation
by One who gave himself
and in the giving
made other answers
immaterial.

12 *hardly Job*

Hardly Job

Not noted
for integrity
intelligence
or visible
assets
and at a loss
for words more often
than not my name
is hardly Job
although I find him kin
in crucial ways.
My littleness is written
large in his heroic
dimensions and my questions
reverberate through heaven
when he shouts them.

Like a Small Job

God gives me room
to rant
and rationalize
to call him names
and listen to the names
I call him.
He has space
to spare
and knows that I
get boxed
or box myself
and need no further
boxing from him.
And it appears
as though he ran—
or flew—away
and left me
chomping my jaws
and listening to my
brilliant expostulations.
"Where have you gone?"
I yell
and think the void
devoid of echoes.
"Answer me now!"
I howl
followed by threats
and pleas for pity
by boasts and bombast
ingenuous ultimatums.
Does he think
I was born yesterday?
Perhaps I was.
But let him show
His face
and I will tell him
a thing or three.

So my suffocation
my madcap turbulence
expatiates
till it subsides
and I am ready
to bow in awe
and wonder at the ways
beyond my wisdom
and welcome him back—
although he had not left me.
Like a small Job
I say
I see!

Could I?

How would I manage
if the woe I see
others enduring
were to mangle me?
How handle the horror
of a damaged child
a cancered parent
or a death prescribed
for soldier son
or suicided friend
or bloody accident
of earth or sky?
How meet the musts
that woe upon the world:
the bombed the poisoned
and the meager fed
the Jobs who have no tally
of their innocence
or their benevolence?
And Job's less righteous brothers
in the human snarl
who cannot correlate
their doom with their deserving?
I think my lips
would stumble if I tried
to equate my natal nakedness
with stripped misfortune
or to balance
God's giving and God's taking.
Could I still
retrieve the *nonetheless* of faith
and say
I bless him.
Could I?

Psalm

O help, O help, O help
me: are the apparently
self-centered words my prayer
spills in an agony of appeal:
O God, O God, O God,
help me, not primarily
my body although that
is where I feel the sharp
danger, not primarily
my mind where the blunt threat
decapitates reason,
but me, O God, O help
me the insignificant,
me the altogether
unworthy petitioner,
O help me, the agonized,
the unanesthetized
soul solitary, O
God help, O God, help me.

13 *Job's question over again*

Job's Question Over Again

My best friends have cancer. They cannot
have contracted it by hatred as some suppose.
They may have been too responsive to growth,
to harboring alien ideas and persons.
At this point in history no one knows
but we all cry for a cure or a retardation
of the spread of the malignant predatory pain.
I would give my life to save them from this death,
I think, but I cannot offer or choose.
They are all part of Job's question over again.
Are there ways they gain while we see them lose?
Is there anything here that may yet be good news?

I Talked With Job

I talked with Job and asked him how he fared
in a world where one man's problems
    are a hundred million's:
not sudden calamity but continued catastrophe,
not unexpected illness but no health,
not a cupboard bitterly depleted
but one never filled or even built,
not children dying for no good reason
but children dead for the maddest and vilest
    of reasons.

I talked with Job and asked him to ask God
what I should do.

Putting It All Together

Weird
    and uncanny
        and a mystery
beyond
    our neat
        profound analysis
our monstrous
    wondrous
        enigmatic world
mixture
    of misery
        and blend of bliss.

And Job Replied

I talked with Job
and asked him how he answered
the agony abroad in God's
occupied Kingdom.
And Job replied:
I once was at
no loss for words
to wise up men
who thought to advise me
with their old
moralities.
At no loss either
to belabor God
for his unjust
assaults on my
tranquility.
Thank God for even
the stupidity
of words that well
from our botched
imaging of him.
It may be
that our cry
is echoing his.

There Was a Man

There was a man
in our vicinity
who in the sight of heaven
and all who ran across him
was christened kind
and gentle
and genuine
and generous
and good
one of God's best
preeminently compassionate
ready to go to jail
to help men read
and write
and hope.
But he went slowly blind.
He lost his job
seeing he could not see
in the acceptable way.
He loved to read
and now and then was read to.
And lying dying
in a hospital
a book club offering came
entitled *JOB*
a story he knew better
than the current author.
He did not curse it
only commented
"And how appropriate!"

By Faith

Her threescore
years and nine
of struggle
and sympathy
and quiet
care and kindness
were crowned
rewarded
and requited
by quick paralysis
and slow decline.
And Job's agenda-ed joy
never materialized
to tranquilize
my mother's misery.

Did He?

Did he need
to suffer
to know
the meaning
of being
a person
the isolate
temptation
to negate
all aspiration
and confide
in nothing
as ultimate
nothing as basically
benevolent?
I speak
of Job
and Jesus
and even the undersigned.

Haunted and Taunted

Job had his Buchenwald
his Lidice
but not at the depraved
design of men.
Whom should he charge
with his dark agony
and would he ever
see the light again?
His questions haunt
the gentleness of heaven
and taunt the world's
claims to benignancy.
If we are given good
are we not given
its opposite
by One who let us *be?*

This Day

Now we will forget
about weather, wars,
and other minor
matters, concentrate
upon our grief,
our unconsolable
concern for all
that ties us to our dying
and sets our current
breathing in relief.

What Good Does It Do Me?

Why be good?
Is it a clever stratagem
to keep God happy and benevolent
and keep the best one has
and harvest more
with no deletions by Divinity?
Is it a means
to sidestep suffering
and to be immune
to ache of tragedy?
Is it to elude—escape—
hell's inconveniences
and lacerations
and eternities?
Or at a given moment
will it provide
protection from the prowl
of guardians of the law?
Is it the path
of least resistance
to enjoyment
of general praise
and approbation?
Would I be good
without a reason
and without reward?
Not likely.
Hardly possible.
What good
can goodness
guarantee
or justify
or generate—
apart from God?

14 the power and the glory forever

Cosmic Clues

Bankrupt and broken and bombarded by
the questions man and God frame for his quest
Job turns his gaze from sty to sky and tries
to drive his Creator to the telling test.
But from the whirlwind's heart his heart is stirred.
The More-than-nature out of nature speaks
the majestic and the all-encompassing word
which points to the perception that he seeks.

Intellection

Job challenged God
unflaggingly demanding
that he listen—
or speak—
and set the record straight.
Great was his faith
that past the apparent absence
God would respond
in his own time and way.

When God Replies

Since you demand of me
that I appear
and answer your
contentious allegations
and try to justify
my ways with you
in lucid terms
from your vocabulary
I might—just might—
surprise you when I do
since you have thought me
silent for so long.
You'll have no better
answers when I'm through
except that I
am still accessible.
I don't forget
the world I set in motion
or those who feel
and image my feelings.

Whirlwind Courtship

With what dark humor
God engages
his quarry
offering counsel
with blockbusters
and thunderbolts
of naturalistic knowledge
watching and waiting
for the sudden turn
the converting moment
when his beloved target
will center and understand
that One who works in wonders
works in him.

Out of the Whirlwind

Within the whirlwind
of eternal mystery
and fantastic
profundity
and inventive power
tinged with tenderness:
the voice
of *I*
to *thou.*

God's Power Play

God's power play
begins to roll
at the appointed signal
of the creative quarterback
who assumes to know
the unpredictable
and inconceivable
rejoinder of him
for whom no man
can speak.

But hear the author through:
The antiphons of thunder
and the roll
of mysteries and marvels
and the raw
beauty of creation
the lines through all the earth
the singing stars
the unstayable sea
the importunate dawn
the antecedents
of rain and snow and ice
the cycles of conception
and the all-provident
balance of nature
the migratory urge
of birds with inbuilt compass
and a south to seek
the mechanics
of behemoth
that masterpiece
lolling beneath the lotus
swallowing rivers
and regurgitating
in the same breath
leviathan too
with terror in his teeth
the impossible pet
the primitive and prodigious
monster sealed in stone
immune to javelins
and the other arms
of men who share with him
the hazards of creation.

Let these be samples
for the speculation
of those who think
to write God's wisdom off
as witless or extinct.

15 Job's children—after

Happy Ending

Maybe there had to be
a happy ending
to get his book
accepted by the Book Club.
God's self-appointed
security guards
might pass the story
on this proper cover
of piety's
precise reward
recorded in
punctilious detail.

Logistics

Job saw double.
His original
losses turned out to be
insured with a divine
indemnity.
Now he kept
an accountant busy
overtime
tallying his assets.
His former friends
decided he was worth
knowing again.
They sure
were sympathetic
brought him gifts
now that he didn't need them.
The wife—who once had wished
him dead or thought that he
should attend to it personally
considering God's unfaithfulness—
supplied him seven sons—
or was that double too?—
names not recorded—
and three spectacular daughters
whom he called
Turtledove
Mascara
and Cinnamon.
It's hard to tell
what all this adds
to the preceding story
except statistics
and a bonus
for those who will not
read a book
or lead a life
without assurance
of a happy ending.

Interview

I questioned Job:
"How did you ever happen
to have such luscious daughters
as their names convey
and as your saga celebrates?
Did they take after you
in courage, eloquence, and wisdom?
What was their mother's
contribution?"

He smiled at my fatuity.

I tried again:
"Why did you choose
to bequeath a handsome share
of your considerable estate
to those whose sex
would ordinarily be
a hopeless handicap
in matters that matter
such as money
and inheritance?"

"I think"—he said—
"I have some sensibility
for what is fair."

16 *the story that never ends*

Another Ashpit

It is a glad spectacle
to find Job sitting
in a different ashpit
in the ultimate chapter.
Conversant still with God.
Still overstocked
with answerless questions
and in spite of words and
      wounds
armed with the bold resolve
to give the lie
to lies of pious prudence.
In ashes
and dust
and dignity
accepting the obscure
design which he himself
obscured in his attempts
to rationalize God's rations.

After the Ashpit

Did Job
dust off
the brittle
grit and ashes
which his sitting
had swaddled him with

shake off
his sorrow
and his centric
anger

expurgate
myopic
passages
of personal
offense

and cock-a-doodle-doo
to God
vociferating
exhilaration
and enthusiasm
for the elusive light
he had just recognized
dawning upon
his raw
hard-boiled
benightedness?

The Glory

And now my eyes
have seen the glory
clarified by pain
and days that even in darkness
delivered happenings
of incidental
illumination
the revelation
of another
dimension to our wonderings
and our wounds.

The Name of Job

The name of Job
is written in the stars
of man's surmising
and his reconstruction
of how he came to know
his brittle ignorance
and feel the profundity
of his affiliation
with mystery
that speaks
confronts
and saves.